PETERHEAD TRAIN

"MAUD—CHANGE FOR FRASERBURGH"

By A. G. Murdoch

To Jacqui and Bobby, who gladden my heart

Other titles in this series:
All Rails Lead to Inverness

and, under preparation
All Rails Lead to Aberdeen

ISBN 0 9519736 0 6

Published by A. G. Murdoch,
21 High Street, Fochabers, Moray IV32 7DX
Printed by BPCC-AUP Aberdeen Ltd.

FOREWORD

Railways made an early impact on my life, when my parents lived in Strichen in 1918. A mere 4½ years old I had strayed from the High Street, and was found by my mother down at the Market Leys, train watching.

Later at Maud School, at dinner break I would give a cursory glance over the dyke as I ran down Station Brae en route to Mrs Maggie Smith for a plate of mince and tatties.

Come 1929, with school behind and three weeks into my apprenticeship with Mr Charles Anderson, I bought my first camera, a Portrait Brownie which clicked on till 1945, and was replaced by a 35mm model with a faster shutter speed.

Train study has changed over the years. When you saw a plume of smoke on the horizon you gave chase and found your quarry, then came the diesels with little clue as to movement.

Now most of the paraffin lit Semaphore signals have been replaced by multi aspect colour lights.

Friendships are forged in pursuit of a common interest and a ready exchange of information is made with complete strangers.

I yield to none in my admiration of railway operative staff, all skilled men and women, be they drivers, signalmen, or track maintenance workers doing their night shift, while the public is all tucked up in bed. At the smaller stations booking office clerks have to operate computerised ticket machines and in addition double as wagon shunters.

In relation to the rest of Europe, British Rail gets the lowest state subsidy. I can only hope that extra funds will be made available in the future.

Peterhead Line closed to passengers on 3/5/65, and for freight 7/9/70.

Fraserburgh Line closed to passengers on 4/10/65 and for freight in October 1979.

My thanks to friends whose help filled some blank spaces. Mr Bruce Ellis, Mr Keith Fenwick, the late Mr Norrie Forrest, Mr Roy Hamilton, and the Archives of the G.N.S.R.A. per Mr Dick Jackson.

A. G. Murdoch,
Fochabers, Moray

ABERDEEN: The exposure was 1/10" Sec as 62276 "Andrew Bain" stands at Platform 12, Joint Station.   22.7.50

ABERDEEN: It was back in 1931 that B12 61504 came north from East Anglia to do a trial run to Peterhead. At the time the G.N.S.R. area required more powerful engines.   May, 1949

5

ABERDEEN: For little boys, Union Terrace Gardens was Utopia. Here B1 61343 draws a crowd as it comes out of Schoolhill Tunnel.   8.8.50

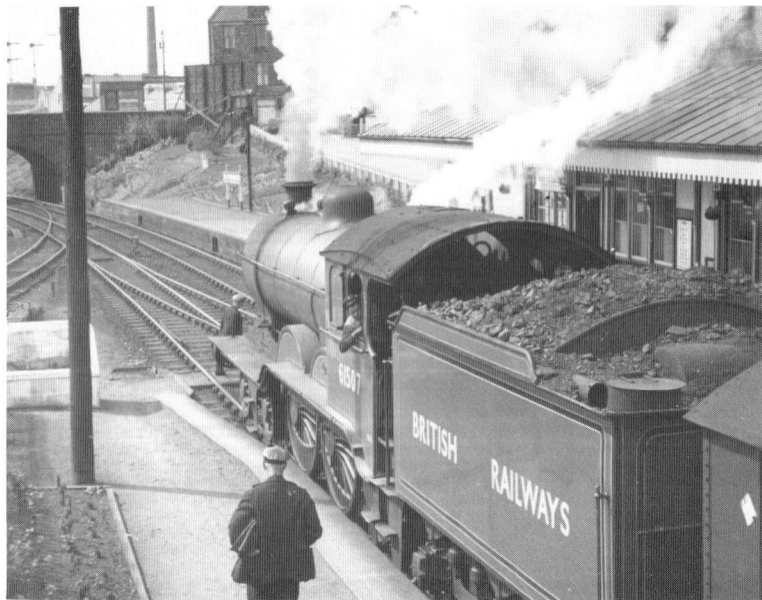

KITTYBREWSTER: Coming home on the cushions was a luxury, after a hard slog on the footplate, especially after an early shift. Crew members pass 61507.

KITTYBREWSTER: No longer is it possible to walk up from the station and catch a tram to St Nicholas Street, or Woodside as this crew might have done, as they finished their shift with B12 4-6-0 61532 in October, 1949.

KITTYBREWSTER: Though its home shed was Ferryhill J35 0-6-0 64485 is seen at Kittybrewster, possibly on a transfer goods.　　11.10.50

7

not till 5/52

KITTYBREWSTER: A fireman's job is never done, next could come raking out of ash, as D40 62279 "Glen Grant" nears its shed.

WOODSIDE: Summer suns are glowing as 62275, named after a director of the G.N.S.R. "Sir David Stewart" hurries north to Dyce.   6.6.50

BUCKSBURN: The former station yard is now covered by a block of flats. Here D40 62273 "George Davidson" heads home for Kittybrewster.

DYCE: This G.N.S.R. wagon was found by the writer in the carriage sheds, and bought for a token sum. It was literally smuggled down by railway staff to the Transport Museum at Falkirk, and now is sited at Bo'ness Railway.

NEWMACHAR: No sign of snow, but steam heat condensing in the cold air as D6143 waits for the Aberdeen train to arrive.

UDNY STATION: 26.036 begins the stiff climb up to Newmachar. The rock cutting to the north of the station was often blocked by snow in the winter.

LOGIERIEVE: The station looking north, the bridge behind carries a cross country road to Newburgh.　　　　　　　　　Photo Keith Fenwick

ESSLEMONT: More of a halt than a station, seen looking towards Logierieve.
Photo Keith Fenwick

ELLON: The track under the bridge leads to Maud Junction, and to the right the Goods Yard and the line to Boddam.   Photo Norrie Forrest

Cruden Bay Hotel.

CRUDEN BAY: An electric tram conveyed passengers and guests from the station to the hotel and adjoining Golf Course.   G.N.S.R.A. Archives

CRUDEN BAY: To the east of the station was a massive viaduct carrying the line to Boddam. At the Up platform is a 'subby' with a train for Ellon.

G.N.S.R.A. Archives

Hatton, from Station

HATTON: This small village has grown and is now a hive of industry. The bakery business started by Mr Simmers is now a subsidiary of United Biscuits, with 250 to 300 of a staff.

BODDAM: All that remained before the station site was cleared and replaced, by quarters for personnel who man R.A.F. Buchan.

ELLON: Type 1 Diesel D8029 comes off the bridge over the River Ythan and heads for Maud Junction.

ELLON: The all round canopy of Ellon Station gave ample shelter to waiting passengers from the rigours of a Buchan winter.   Photo Norrie Forrest

ARNAGE: The negative actions of Beeching closures already shows as N.B. D6150 goes north with traffic for Maud.   6.7.65

15

AUCHNAGATT: Passenger numbers did not warrant this station having two signal boxes. N.B. D6153 waits to proceed as Cravens Twin D.M.U. Se 51480 arrives with an Aberdeen train.   6.7.65

AUCHNAGATT: Local pupils got higher grade schooling at Maud, and secondary education at Ellon. D41 6904 calls on its return journey to Aberdeen.   May 1931

MAUD JUNCTION: The tail light on the tender of B12 61543 is an indication to signalmen and means the locomotive is travelling back to Kittybrewster without a load.   19.7.50

MAUD: Tuesday afternoon as D41 62230 negotiates the points with a train of empty trucks which will be filled with livestock from the auction sale next day.

MAUD: The second man does a leisurely exchange of tokens, as Type 2 D5070 drifts down the grade on its way to Peterhead.

MAUD: Peterhead bound D6141 piloting D6150 arrives from Aberdeen on a cold winters day. Banff and Buchan Council have restored the former station building and made what was the booking office into a museum of railway relics.   1.3.65

MINTLAW: Clayton class 18 D8604 passes the Abbey Gardens, Old Deer. Traffic proceeding to Aberdeen 'Light Diesel' could at times indicate a poor landing of fish.

MINTLAW: D6139 collects some coal empties. The token exchange apparatus seen recessed in front of the cab door enabled trains to pass through stations without stopping.   5.4.65

MINTLAW: Type 1 EE. D8006 in the shape of things to c

ets 2-6-4T 80114 on its way to Peterhead from Aberdeen.

MINTLAW: The breakdown crane from Kittybrewster came to the rescue of 2-6-4T 80004 which got derailed while shunting.

MINTLAW: As the train stops, the guard walks up the platform shunting pole in hand, ready to couple up empty wagons on the siding.

LONGSIDE: No high speed train 2MT 2-6-0 78045 saunters up past Crooked Neuk with an afternoon train from Peterhead.

LONGSIDE: First class travel was never a winner in Buchan, passengers much preferred to have a "news" with fellow travellers. D6157 is seen departing for Peterhead. 5.8.65

NEWSEAT: A wayside halt, but very busy during the last war with, servicemen and women from the adjoining Aerodrome, and now a heliport.

July 1969. Photo Keith Fenwick

INVERUGIE: Was and still is a desirable residential suburb of Peterhead.

July 1969. Photo Keith Fenwick

PETERHEAD: (R) Signalman Jim Simpson of Maud, who previously served at Long Carse before being posted home when the box closed. 5.8.65

PETERHEAD: B1 4-6-0 61401 all spic and span seen ready to depart for Aberdeen with a Crosse and Blackwell Goods. Peterhead Academy now covers this site.

PETERHEAD: Mr Alex Watt a well kent face on the Peterhead-Aberdeen run. He had great patience with the worthies finishing their 'nips' at Maud refresh, before giving a driver the green flag.

photo courtesy his daughter

PETERHEAD: The Claytons were underpowered and on the main line operated in pairs. They had one plus point, an electric hob for the crew. D8616 shunts the yard.

PETERHEAD: 2P 4-4-0 40603 (former L.M.S. Loco) was at Kittybrewster from 1948 till 1961. Postwar housing progress can be gauged by the very few houses of Balmoor Terrace seen behind the engine.

PETERHEAD: Just time for a quick brew up before D6157 gets under way for Maud and Aberdeen.   5.8.65

MAUD: The sloping roof behind the tender of D40 62271 marks the pharmacy built by the late Mr Charles Anderson with whom I served my apprenticeship from 1929–1933.

MAUD: Wednesday at Maud as 2P 40622 blasts off with a goods train from Fraserburgh, and B1 61307 waits for the cattle wagons to fill.   30.8.50

MAUD: In much a like manner as their flesh and blood equivalents would have done, iron horses 62262 and 62278 "Hatton Castle" have a tete a tete before departure.

MAUD: Originally designed by Fairburn for L.M.S. passenger work, this stray 2-6-4T 4T 42689 was on goods duty.   August 1949

MAUD: Fresh Herring! B1 61307 comes through non stop with a big landing from
the Broch being rushed to Aberdeen in time for the 2 o'clock to Billingsgate.

B12 61532 ?

MAUD: Former North British loco D31 4-4-0 62065 spent two years at 'Kitty'
before being blowtorched at Inverurie in 1949.

MAUD: Mr Willie Joss parks his trolley as the driver of D5357 waits for the 'away' on his run down to Fraserburgh.

MAUD: The increase in the gradient reduces the speed of N.B. D6145 as it nears the station with a load of containers, possibly holding compressors from the Toolworks, Fraserburgh.

BRUCKLAY: With just sufficient head of steam to take it over the top at Atherb 62065 can then coast down the hill for a breather at Maud. 1948

BRUCKLAY: The sun was still in the east when D41 62228 arrived with 9.40 a.m. for Fraserburgh 11.5.50

STRICHEN: The sign of a good fireman, just a feather of steam from the safety valve, and no black smoke as D40 62272 nears the summit, and on to Brucklay.

STRICHEN: Once across the Ugie Bridge, D40 62268 picks up speed to take it past the Brewery and up the 1 in 60 gradient to the west of Strichen House.

STRICHEN: N.B. Diesel 6138 gives off a cloud of black exhaust as the driver turns on power in a shunting movement.

STRICHEN: Where it all began. The driver of this engine waits to cross a passenger train arriving from Aberdeen.

MORMOND: The G.N.S.R. directorate must have been super optimists to think that this station would ever pay its way. 27011 passes on its way to Strichen.

LONMAY: The axe had fallen and this station's decline had started D6156 stops with the 18.10 hrs ex Aberdeen. 6.7.65

RATHEN: The shadows get longer as Class 25 D5124 passes Rathen with an evening train to Aberdeen.

PHILORTH HALT: Originally a private station for Lord Saltoun of Cairnbulg Castle, but later made available to the public. 1990

CAIRNBULG: This station was of an identical plan to the one at St. Combs. Class F4 2-4-2 T 67151 arrives. photo A. G. Ellis Collection

ST. COMBS: Classified a light railway, parts of the line had no fencing so that engines had to be fitted with a cowcatcher as seen on 2MT 2-6-0 46460. photo Roy Hamilton

FRASERBURGH: When this photo was taken only the goods service remained.
25011 makes up its load for Aberdeen.

FRASERBURGH: In the bleak midwinter overcoats are very welcome. Compared to
steam days the crew of D6148 will travel to Aberdeen in comfort.

FRASERBURGH: Drivers hand on the throttle as F4 67164 marshals the trucks in the adjoining sidings. 20.7.50

FRASERBURGH: Busy scene at the Broch, Class 2P 46460 prepares to couple up a loose wagon as a 2-6-4T leaves for Aberdeen with a mixed train.

FRASERBURGH: The engine shed behind the locomotive is all that remains of Fraserburgh Station. D40 62261 is on the turntable.

June 1949

FRASERBURGH: The cost of manpower and maintenance led to the demise of steam. Compared to 67151 and 62229 in the rear, diesels did not have to go to Kittybrewster for a boiler wash out every 7 to 10 days.